Cooking with Max Mariola: A Culinary Adventure

Discover the Best of Italian Cuisine, Classic Meals, Culinary Secrets and Signature Recipes from Italy's Top Chef.

Caitlyn C. Sherrill

Copyright © Caitlyn C. Sherrill 2024.

All Rights Reserved.

Before making any copies or reproductions of this document in any manner, it is essential to secure permission from the publisher. Therefore, the contents within cannot be electronically archived, transferred, or stored in a database without prior authorization. Furthermore, no part of this document, be it the entire content or any segment thereof, may be duplicated, scanned, faxed, or retained without explicit approval from the publisher or the document's creator.

Table of Contents

Introduction 8

Chapter 1 10
Max Mariola and his culinary philosophy 10
   The history of Italian cuisine 12
   The importance of Italian cuisine in the world .. 13

Chapter 2 16
Max Mariola's Kitchen Secrets 16
   Max Mariola's unique approach to cooking 16
   His signature techniques 19
   Tips on how to incorporate these techniques into your own cooking.. 21

Chapter 3 24
Classic Italian Dishes 24
   The history and significance of classic Italian dishes.. 24
   Recipes for Max Mariola's favorite classic Italian dishes.. 26
      Spaghetti alla Carbonara 26
      Margherita Pizza 27

Tiramisu 28
   Pasta alla Norma 30
   Saltimbocca alla Romana 31
   Risotto alla Milanese 32
   Pesto alla Genovese 33
   Salt-Crusted Branzino 34
 Unique twists on classic Italian dishes 35

Chapter 4 39
Contemporary Italian Cuisine 39
 The evolution of Italian cuisine 39
 Max Mariola's contemporary Italian dishes 41
   Spinach and Ricotta Ravioli 41
   Dan Pepperell's Fried Chicken alla Diavola .. 43
   Capitano's Sugarsnap Pea "Scapece" 45
   Guy Grossi's Pearl Barley Polenta 47
   Acme's Maltagliati with Washed Kimchi and Guanciale 48
   Pinbone's Hazelnut Tiramisù 50
   Parmesan Chawanmushi 52
   Carpaccio of Kangaroo with Beetroot and Native Fruits 54
   Swordfish con Sarde 56
   Popolo's Frittata "Carbonara" 58

Max Mariola favorite contemporary Italian dishes 60

   Smoked Eel Carbonara 60

   Pici Bolognese with Fish Sauce 62

   Roasted Crispy Broccoli with Parmigiano Reggiano and Garlic 63

   Burrata and Tomato Salad 65

   Pork Milanese with Arugula Salad 66

Chapter 5 69

Pasta and Risotto 69

   Importance of pasta and risotto in Italian cuisine. 69

   Max Mariola's favorite pasta and risotto dishes. 71

      Spaghetti with Clams and Mussels 71

      Saffron Spaghetti Cooked Risotto-Style 73

      Pesto Risotto with Roasted Tomatoes 74

      Risotto with Asparagus and Crescenza Cheese 76

      Pasta with Cime di Rapa and Totani 78

      Pasta with Fungi Cardoncelli and Salsiccia ... 79

Chapter 6 81
Seafood 81
  Importance of seafood in Italian cuisine 81
  Max Mariola's favorite seafood dishes 83
    Linguine allo Scoglio 83
    Fritto Misto di Pesce 84
    Spaghetti alle Vongole 85
    Linguine all'Astice: 86
    Risotto ai Frutti di Mare 87

Chapter 7 89
Meat and Poultry 89
  Importance of meat and poultry in Italian cuisine
  89
  Max Mariola's favorite meat and poultry dishes 92
    Osso Buco 92
    Pollo alla Cacciatora 93
    Bistecca alla Fiorentina 94
    Porchetta 96
    Arrosto di Maiale (Italian Roast Pork) 97
  Unique twists on classic meat and poultry dishes
  98

Chapter 8 .... **100**
Vegetarian and Vegan Dishes **100**

   Importance of vegetarian and vegan dishes in Italian cuisine 100

   Max Mariola's favorite vegetarian and vegan dishes 102

      Pesto 102

      Minestrone 103

      Bruschetta 104

      Risotto ai Funghi 105

Chapter 9 .... **107**
Desserts **107**

   Importance of desserts in Italian cuisine 107

   Max Mariola's favorite Italian desserts 109

      Sicilian Cassata 109

      Neapolitan Sfogliatella 110

      Venetian Torte 111

   Unique twists on classic Italian desserts 113

Conclusion **115**

Introduction

Hop on a culinary journey that transcends the boundaries of taste and tradition – welcome to ***"Cooking with Max Mariola: A Culinary Adventure."*** In the heart of this gastronomic exploration lies a fusion of flavors, a celebration of simplicity, and a testament to the profound connection between food and culture. If you've ever yearned to ***master the art of Italian cooking***, guided by the expertise of renowned chef Max Mariola, then this book is your passport to a world where every meal is a work of passion.

Max Mariola, a maestro of contemporary Italian cuisine, unveils the secrets behind his visually stunning and delectable creations. From classic Roman dishes to inventive, modern twists, Max's culinary prowess is a tapestry woven with the history of Italy, the innovation of the present, and the promise of an extraordinary dining experience.

I invite you to savor the essence of Italy, one dish at a time. In this adventure, we'll explore the foundational principles of Max's cooking philosophy, discover the intricate history of Italian cuisine, and unravel the contemporary twists on beloved classics. Join me as we navigate the diverse landscapes of pasta, risotto, seafood, meats, and vegetarian delights, uncovering the unique twists that set Max's dishes apart.

But this journey is more than just a collection of recipes; it's a celebration of the Italian way of life. Through the pages of this book, we'll not only delve into the artistry of Max Mariola but also gain insights into the cultural tapestry that defines each bite. You'll learn how fresh, high-quality ingredients, passion, and creativity are the cornerstones of this culinary adventure.

Fear not, for this is not a daunting expedition. I am both your expert writing coach and trusted chef, ready to guide you through every step. From the simplicity of Pici Bolognese to the elegance of Osso Buco, we'll conquer the kitchen together.

So, fasten your aprons, sharpen your knives, and let's embark on "Cooking with Max Mariola: A Culinary Adventure." A tantalizing world of flavors awaits, where every recipe is a chapter, and every bite is a page turned in the captivating story of Italian gastronomy. Get ready to elevate your cooking skills and savor the magic of Max's kitchen.

Buon viaggio culinario!!!!

Chapter 1

Max Mariola and his culinary philosophy.

Max Mariola, a distinguished figure in the world of Italian cuisine, boasts a remarkable career spanning over three decades as a chef and consultant across various culinary platforms, including restaurants, hotels, and cooking channels. Throughout his journey, Max has solidified his reputation as an innovative force, contributing significantly to the culinary landscape.

At the core of Max Mariola's culinary ethos lies a profound belief in simplicity. He advocates for cherishing the inherent qualities of ingredients, be they products of nature or human cultivation, without succumbing to unnecessary complexities. Max's culinary compass is guided by the principle of not spoiling the essence of ingredients but rather enhancing them with heart and sincerity.

Intrinsically tied to Max's culinary philosophy is the promotion of quality Made in Italy cuisine on a global scale. Max Mariola, through his unique culinary approach, seeks to showcase the richness and authenticity of Italian gastronomy to the world. His dedication to this cause has positioned him as a prominent ambassador of Italian culinary excellence.

Max's cooking style revolves around a commitment to simplicity. He firmly believes that the finest dishes are crafted from fresh, high-quality ingredients, handled with care, and prepared with meticulous attention to detail. Embracing straightforward techniques, Max allows the natural flavors of the ingredients to take center stage in his creations. His signature methods include the judicious use of fresh herbs and spices, along with techniques such as grilling and roasting, which contribute to the distinctive character of his culinary creations.

Beyond technique, Max Mariola draws inspiration from the historical tapestry of Italian cuisine. He perceives Italian culinary traditions as a mirror reflecting the nation's rich cultural heritage. To Max, preserving this heritage is not merely a culinary duty but a cultural responsibility. His passion for classic Italian dishes is palpable, underpinned by a profound understanding of their historical significance.

Max Mariola emerges as a celebrated Italian chef, whose culinary journey spans decades of rich experiences. Grounded in simplicity, quality, and a deep appreciation for the historical roots of Italian cuisine, Max's innovative approach showcases his commitment to letting the natural essence of ingredients shine through. Whether through the use of fresh herbs, spices, grilling, or roasting, Max Mariola's culinary artistry is a testament to the enduring allure of authentic and straightforward Italian gastronomy.

The history of Italian cuisine

The story of Italian cuisine is a captivating journey through time, a tale woven with the threads of history, culture, and the vibrant flavors of the most extraordinary recipes. It is a narrative that unfolds over centuries, mirroring the evolution and transformations of Italy amidst wars, cultural shifts, and diverse influences.

Rooted in the ancient history of Rome, Italian cuisine traces its origins back to the 4th century BC, offering a glimpse into a culinary heritage that has stood the test of time. The cookbook "Apicius," a culinary relic from the first century BC, attests to the profound connection between food and culture during this era. The Romans, enamored with the art of feasting, turned banquets into more than just moments of social camaraderie; they became arenas where new culinary creations were introduced and savored.

As Italy weathered the storms of centuries, Italian cuisine evolved hand in hand with the nation's own metamorphosis. Wars, cultural revolutions, and cross-cultural exchanges left indelible imprints on the culinary landscape. The history of Italian cuisine unfolds as a riveting narrative, featuring not only the exquisite flavors of recipes but also the traditions, royal influences, and the resilience of a people molded by the challenges of their times.

The history of Italian cuisine is a saga that transcends the kitchen, intertwining with the broader tapestry of Italy's past. It is a tale of food, traditions, the reigns of kings, and the valor of warriors, presented in a manner as rich and enthralling as the most extraordinary recipes that have graced Italian tables through the ages.

Italian cuisine boasts a deep-rooted and vibrant history, dating back to the days of the Roman Empire. This culinary tradition has weathered the tides of change, evolving alongside the dynamic history of Italy itself. The story of Italian cuisine is a captivating blend of food, traditions, and cultural shifts, echoing through the ages with the allure of the most remarkable recipes.

The importance of Italian cuisine in the world

Italian cuisine stands as a global culinary powerhouse, cherished and adored by people worldwide. The reasons behind its prominence and influence are as diverse and flavorful as the dishes it presents.

Tradition:

At the heart of Italian cuisine lies a rich tapestry of tradition. Passed down through generations of Italian families, many of the dishes that grace our tables today carry the echoes of a culinary heritage steeped in history. This longstanding tradition is not merely a collection of recipes; it's a testament to the resilience of unique flavors and time-honored techniques that define Italian gastronomy.

Quality:

Italian cuisine is synonymous with a commitment to excellence in ingredients. From the crisp freshness of herbs and vegetables to the artisanal craftsmanship behind cheeses and meats, the emphasis on using high-quality, fresh ingredients is a hallmark of Italian culinary artistry. This dedication to quality has elevated Italian cuisine to a pedestal of respect and admiration on the global stage.

Variety:

Diversity is a cornerstone of Italian cuisine, offering a delightful spectrum of options to suit every palate. Whether savoring classic pasta dishes or indulging in hearty meat-based creations, Italian cuisine unfolds like a gastronomic adventure with a myriad of flavors and textures. This variety is a key factor that has contributed to the widespread appeal and popularity of Italian cuisine worldwide.

Influence:

Italian cuisine's impact extends far beyond its own borders, having left an indelible mark on global culinary practices. Techniques and ingredients unique to Italian cooking have been warmly adopted by diverse cultures and cuisines. This far-reaching influence has positioned Italian cuisine as not just important but as a true cornerstone in the global culinary landscape.

Conviviality:

More than just a feast for the taste buds, Italian cuisine places a premium on the social experience of sharing meals with loved ones. The conviviality that accompanies Italian dining reflects a cultural value placed on communal enjoyment. This emphasis on togetherness has played a pivotal role in making Italian cuisine not just a culinary delight but an emotional and social celebration.

The significance and influence of Italian cuisine stem from a blend of rich tradition, unwavering commitment to quality, a diverse array of flavors, far-reaching global influence, and a heartfelt emphasis on conviviality. It's this unique combination that has propelled Italian cuisine to its status as one of the most cherished and globally beloved culinary traditions.

Chapter 2

Max Mariola's Kitchen Secrets

Max Mariola's unique approach to cooking

Max Mariola, a luminary in the world of Italian cuisine, carries a culinary legacy spanning over three decades, earning him acclaim as a celebrated chef. At the core of Max's culinary philosophy lies a commitment to simplicity, a profound connection to the essence of ingredients, and a heartfelt appreciation for the craftsmanship of nature and human cultivation.

Experience and Expertise:

With an impressive tenure of over 30 years in the culinary industry, Max Mariola stands as a seasoned maestro in the art of cooking. His wealth of experience encompasses diverse roles, from the kitchens of renowned restaurants to consultancy in the hospitality sector and contributions to cooking channels. This journey has honed Max's skills, solidifying his reputation as an innovative force in Italian cuisine.

Simplicity and Heartfelt Connection:

Max's culinary ideology revolves around the simplicity of preparation and a genuine appreciation for the origins of ingredients. For him, the heart of a dish lies in cherishing what nature and humans have cultivated. This philosophy underscores his belief that the most exceptional dishes are born from the use of fresh, high-quality ingredients, handled with care, and crafted with meticulous attention to detail.

Signature Techniques:

Max is renowned for his distinctive culinary techniques, each contributing to the unique character of his creations. From the judicious use of fresh herbs and spices to the art of grilling and roasting, Max's signature methods are a testament to his innovative approach to cooking. These techniques, rather than being mere embellishments, serve to enhance and amplify the inherent flavors of the ingredients.

Culinary Heritage and Passion for Tradition:

Max Mariola's culinary journey is deeply intertwined with the rich tapestry of Italian cuisine's history. He sees Italian culinary traditions not only as a reflection of the country's cultural heritage but as a responsibility to preserve and promote traditional dishes. Max's passion for classic Italian fare is palpable, grounded in a profound understanding of the historical significance of these dishes.

Simple and Elegant Creations:

Max's unique prowess lies in his ability to craft dishes that are simultaneously simple and elegant. His culinary creations are a delicate balance, allowing the natural flavors of the ingredients to take center stage. Max's approach rejects complexity, favoring simple techniques that amplify the inherent qualities of each component, steering clear of the obscuring veil of complex sauces or overpowering seasonings.

Max Mariola's culinary persona is a fusion of experience, simplicity, and a deep reverence for Italy's culinary legacy. His signature techniques, grounded in fresh ingredients and simple preparation, showcase not only his expertise but also a commitment to allowing the true essence of flavors to shine through. Max's culinary journey is a testament to the enduring allure of Italian cuisine, where each dish becomes a celebration of simplicity, quality, and a profound respect for history.

His signature techniques

Max Mariola's culinary prowess extends beyond the mere preparation of dishes; it is an art form, a symphony of flavors, colors, and creativity that culminates in visually stunning and utterly delicious creations. At the heart of Mariola's signature technique is a unique ability to transform fresh, high-quality ingredients into culinary masterpieces, elevating the dining experience to a feast for both the eyes and the palate.

Visual Splendor and Bold Flavors:

Mariola's dishes are a feast for the senses, characterized by bold flavors that dance on the taste buds and vibrant colors that captivate the eye. Each plate is a canvas, meticulously crafted to showcase the ingredients' natural beauty. This visual splendor is not a mere afterthought but an integral part of Mariola's culinary philosophy, where the aesthetics of a dish are as important as its taste.

Innovative Combinations:

What sets Mariola apart is his ability to think outside the culinary box. He ingeniously combines ingredients in ways that surprise and delight, creating harmonious flavor profiles that elevate the dining experience. The creativity in his combinations is not just about novelty; it's a deliberate exploration of flavors that challenges the conventional boundaries of taste.

Creamy Sauce Technique:

One standout element in Mariola's repertoire is his unique technique for crafting creamy sauces. This culinary secret adds a layer of sophistication to his dishes, as he skillfully balances textures and flavors. Whether drizzling a velvety sauce over a savory dish or infusing it with a hint of richness, Mariola's mastery of this technique enhances the overall dining experience.

Versatility Across Dishes:

Mariola's signature technique is not confined to a specific dish or cuisine. It is an overarching philosophy that permeates all his creations. He believes that cooking is an art form, a canvas upon which flavors are painted with passion, creativity, and an intimate understanding of the ingredients. This approach results in dishes that transcend the ordinary, offering a culinary experience that resonates with both connoisseurs and casual diners alike.

Passion, Creativity, and Understanding:

For Max Mariola, the essence of culinary excellence lies in the triumvirate of passion, creativity, and a deep understanding of ingredients. This trinity guides his every move in the kitchen, ensuring that each dish is not merely a composition of flavors but a testament to the artistry of cooking. Mariola's belief in the transformative power of these elements shines through in every dish he presents to his patrons.

Max Mariola's signature technique is a multifaceted expression of culinary artistry. From visually stunning presentations to bold flavors and innovative combinations, his approach is a testament to the belief that cooking is more than a practical skill—it's a form of art that engages the senses and elevates the dining experience to a realm of pure delight.

Tips on how to incorporate these techniques into your own cooking

Max Mariola's culinary artistry, renowned for its combination of visual splendor and delectable flavors, has garnered admiration from enthusiasts and novices alike. His signature technique, rooted in the use of fresh, high-quality ingredients and a creative approach to their combination, transforms ordinary meals into extraordinary culinary experiences. Here are practical tips to infuse Mariola's techniques into your own cooking, creating dishes that are not only a treat for the taste buds but also a feast for the eyes.

Embrace Fresh, High-Quality Ingredients:

Mariola's culinary journey begins with the selection of top-notch ingredients. To replicate his success, prioritize using fresh, high-quality produce. Opt for seasonal and locally sourced items, ensuring your dishes burst with vibrant flavors and essential nutrients. Mariola's emphasis on quality ingredients sets the foundation for a memorable dining experience.

Experiment with Flavor Combinations:

Mariola's genius lies in his fearless experimentation with flavor combinations. Break free from the ordinary and dare to pair sweet with savory or infuse a hint of spice into sour elements. Play with contrasting tastes to discover unexpected harmonies. This creativity in the kitchen allows you to craft dishes that surprise and delight, much like Mariola's own creations.

Elevate Presentation:

A hallmark of Mariola's dishes is their intricate and visually appealing presentation. To emulate this, shift your focus beyond taste alone. Experiment with plating techniques, incorporating colorful ingredients to create visually stunning dishes. Remember, the eyes often feast before the mouth, and a well-presented dish heightens the overall dining experience.

Practice Culinary Artistry:

Mariola views cooking as an art form, a canvas to be painted with passion, creativity, and a deep understanding of ingredients. To truly embody his signature technique, embrace cooking as a form of self-expression. Practice, make mistakes, and refine your skills. The more you immerse yourself in the culinary process, the closer you come to capturing the essence of Mariola's approach.

Integrating Max Mariola's signature techniques into your own cooking is a journey of exploration and enhancement. By prioritizing fresh, high-quality ingredients, experimenting with unique flavor combinations, focusing on presentation, and embracing culinary artistry through practice, you elevate your skills. The result is dishes that not only please the palate but also captivate the eyes—a culinary achievement sure to leave a lasting impression.

Chapter 3

Classic Italian Dishes

The history and significance of classic Italian dishes

Italian cuisine is known for its rich history and cultural significance. The cuisine has evolved and changed following the evolution and changes of Italy itself throughout centuries of wars, cultural mutations, and contacts 1. Italian cuisine is a delicious melting pot of flavors and cultures hailing from every corner of the Earth, the heritage and history of which is usually well rooted into the community.

The history of Italian cuisine is as long and rich as the country's history itself, its origins laying deep into the ancestral history of Rome, its people, and its political, cultural, and social power. The Roman Empire and the early Middle Ages were a time when the banquet was not simply a moment of social conviviality, but also the place where new dishes were served and tried. The Renaissance period saw the emergence of new ingredients and techniques, which led to the creation of many classic Italian dishes that are still popular today.

Classic Italian dishes are known for their simplicity and use of fresh, high-quality ingredients. Some of the most famous Italian dishes include pizza, pasta, risotto, and lasagna. Pizza, which originated in Naples, is a flatbread that is topped with tomato sauce, cheese, and various toppings. Pasta is a staple food in Italian cuisine and is typically made from wheat flour and water. It is often served with a variety of sauces, including tomato sauce, pesto, and Alfredo sauce. Risotto is a creamy rice dish that is typically made with Arborio rice, chicken broth, and Parmesan cheese. Lasagna is a layered pasta dish that is typically made with ground meat, tomato sauce, and cheese.

These classic Italian dishes have become popular all over the world and are often associated with Italian cuisine. They are known for their delicious flavors, fresh ingredients, and cultural significance. Italian cuisine is a reflection of Italy's rich history and cultural heritage, and continues to be an important part of Italian culture today.

Recipes for Max Mariola's favorite classic Italian dishes

Spaghetti alla Carbonara

This classic Roman dish is made with spaghetti, eggs, pancetta, and Pecorino Romano cheese. It is a simple yet delicious dish that is perfect for a quick and easy dinner.

Here's a recipe that serves 4 people:

Ingredients:

- 1 pound spaghetti
- 4 large eggs
- 1/2 cup grated Pecorino Romano cheese
- 1/2 cup grated Parmesan cheese
- 8 ounces pancetta or bacon, diced
- 4 cloves garlic, minced
- Salt and pepper to taste

Directions:

- Cook the spaghetti according to the package instructions until al dente.
- While the spaghetti is cooking, whisk together the eggs, Pecorino Romano cheese, and Parmesan cheese in a bowl.
- In a large skillet, cook the pancetta or bacon over medium heat until crispy. Add the garlic and cook for an additional minute.

- Drain the spaghetti and add it to the skillet with the pancetta. Toss to combine.
- Remove the skillet from the heat and add the egg mixture. Toss to combine until the eggs are cooked and the sauce is creamy.
- Season with salt and pepper to taste and serve immediately.

Margherita Pizza

This classic Neapolitan pizza is made with tomato sauce, fresh mozzarella cheese, and basil.

Here's a recipe that serves 4 people:

Ingredients:

- 1 pound pizza dough
- 1/2 cup tomato sauce
- 8 ounces fresh mozzarella cheese, sliced
- 1/4 cup fresh basil leaves
- Salt and pepper to taste

Directions:

- Preheat the oven to 450°F.
- Roll out the pizza dough on a floured surface to your desired thickness.
- Spread the tomato sauce evenly over the pizza dough.
- Arrange the mozzarella cheese slices over the tomato sauce.

- Bake the pizza in the preheated oven for 10-12 minutes, or until the crust is golden brown and the cheese is melted and bubbly.
- Remove the pizza from the oven and sprinkle with fresh basil leaves.
- Season with salt and pepper to taste and serve immediately.

Tiramisu

This classic Italian dessert is made with ladyfingers, espresso, mascarpone cheese, and cocoa powder.

Here's a recipe that serves 6 people:

Ingredients:

- 6 egg yolks
- 3/4 cup white sugar
- 2/3 cup milk
- 1 1/4 cups heavy cream
- 1/2 teaspoon vanilla extract
- 1 pound mascarpone cheese
- 1/4 cup strong brewed espresso, cooled
- 2 tablespoons rum
- 24 ladyfingers
- 2 tablespoons cocoa powder

Directions:

- In a medium saucepan, whisk together the egg yolks and sugar until well blended. Whisk in the milk and cook over low heat, stirring constantly, until the mixture thickens and coats the back of a spoon.
- Remove the saucepan from the heat and let the mixture cool to room temperature.
- In a large bowl, beat the heavy cream and vanilla extract until stiff peaks form.
- In another large bowl, beat the mascarpone cheese until smooth. Fold in the whipped cream.
- In a small bowl, combine the espresso and rum.
- Dip each ladyfinger into the espresso mixture and arrange them in a single layer in the bottom of a 9x13 inch dish.
- Spread half of the mascarpone mixture over the ladyfingers. Repeat with another layer of ladyfingers and mascarpone mixture.
- Cover the dish with plastic wrap and refrigerate for at least 2 hours, or overnight.
- Before serving, dust the top of the tiramisu with cocoa powder.

Pasta alla Norma

Servings: 4

Ingredients:

- 400g rigatoni pasta
- 2 eggplants
- 400g canned tomatoes
- 1 onion, chopped
- 2 cloves garlic, minced
- 100g ricotta salata cheese
- Fresh basil
- Salt and pepper
- Olive oil

Directions:

- Preheat the oven to 200°C.
- Cut the eggplants into small cubes and place them in a colander. Sprinkle with salt and let them sit for 30 minutes.
- Rinse the eggplants and pat them dry.
- In a pan, heat some olive oil over medium heat. Add the onion and garlic and cook until softened.
- Add the canned tomatoes and eggplants. Simmer for 20 minutes.
- Cook the rigatoni pasta in salted boiling water until al dente.
- Drain the pasta and add it to the pan with the tomato sauce. Toss to combine.

- Serve with crumbled ricotta salata cheese and fresh basil leaves.

Saltimbocca alla Romana

Servings: 4

Ingredients:

- 4 veal cutlets
- 8 slices of prosciutto
- 8 fresh sage leaves
- Flour
- Salt and pepper
- Olive oil
- 1/2 cup white wine

Directions:

- Place a slice of prosciutto and a sage leaf on each veal cutlet. Secure with a toothpick.
- Season the cutlets with salt and pepper and dust with flour.
- In a pan, heat some olive oil over medium heat. Add the cutlets and cook for 2-3 minutes on each side.
- Add the white wine to the pan and let it simmer for a few minutes.
- Remove the toothpicks and serve hot.

Risotto alla Milanese

Servings: 4

Ingredients:

- 320g Carnaroli rice
- 1 onion, chopped
- 1.5L chicken broth
- 1/2 cup white wine
- 100g grated Parmesan cheese
- 50g butter
- 1 sachet of saffron
- Salt and pepper
- Olive oil

Directions:

- In a pan, heat some olive oil over medium heat. Add the onion and cook until softened.
- Add the rice and toast for a few minutes.
- Add the white wine and let it evaporate.
- Add a ladleful of chicken broth and stir until absorbed.
- Continue adding the broth, one ladleful at a time, stirring constantly, until the rice is cooked al dente.
- In a small bowl, dissolve the saffron in a ladleful of broth.

- Add the saffron to the risotto and stir to combine. 8. Remove from the heat and add the Parmesan cheese and butter. Stir until melted.
- Season with salt and pepper.
- Serve hot.

Pesto alla Genovese

Servings: 4

Ingredients:

- 400g trofie pasta
- 2 cups fresh basil leaves
- 1/2 cup grated Parmesan cheese
- 1/2 cup grated Pecorino cheese
- 1/2 cup pine nuts
- 2 cloves garlic
- 1/2 cup olive oil
- Salt and pepper

Directions:

- Cook the trofie pasta in salted boiling water until al dente.
- In a food processor, combine the basil leaves, Parmesan cheese, Pecorino cheese, pine nuts, garlic, salt, and pepper. Pulse until finely chopped.

- With the food processor running, slowly pour in the olive oil until the pesto is smooth.
- Drain the pasta and add it to a bowl. Add the pesto and toss to combine.
- Serve hot.

Salt-Crusted Branzino

Servings: 4

Ingredients:

- 2 whole branzino, cleaned and scaled
- 4 cups coarse sea salt
- 4 egg whites
- 1 lemon, sliced
- 1/2 cup fresh parsley, chopped
- 1/2 cup fresh thyme, chopped
- Olive oil
- Salt and pepper

Directions:

- Preheat the oven to 200°C.
- In a bowl, mix together the sea salt, egg whites, parsley, and thyme.
- Stuff the cavity of each branzino with lemon slices and season with salt and pepper.

- Spread half of the salt mixture on the bottom of a baking dish. Place the branzino on top of the salt mixture.
- Cover the branzino with the remaining salt mixture, making sure it is completely covered.
- Bake in the oven for 20-25 minutes.
- Remove from the oven and let it rest for 5 minutes.
- Crack open the salt crust and remove the branzino. Drizzle with olive oil and serve hot.

Unique twists on classic Italian dishes

In the ever-evolving world of culinary innovation, contemporary spins on classic Italian dishes are capturing the imaginations of chefs and home cooks alike. This exciting trend involves introducing new ingredients, techniques, and flavors to traditional recipes, resulting in a delightful fusion of familiarity and novelty. Let's explore some noteworthy examples of these modern twists on classic Italian dishes, where creativity takes center stage.

Cannoli Chips & Dip:

The beloved Italian dessert, cannoli, undergoes a playful transformation with Cannoli Chips & Dip. Departing from the traditional stuffed cannoli, chefs are opting to turn the delectable filling into a dip. Picture triangular pieces of the cannoli shell transformed into chips, perfect for sharing with friends. This inventive take introduces a communal aspect to the indulgent sweetness of the classic dessert.

Polenta Fries:

Polenta, a versatile Italian ingredient, steps into a new role as the star of Polenta Fries. Reminiscent of golden French fries, these sticks of polenta can be grilled, baked, or fried to perfection. Dipped in ketchup, garlic aioli, or other flavorful condiments, polenta fries offer a whimsical twist on a traditional dish, adding a crispy and savory element to the Italian culinary repertoire.

Meatball Bake:

Meatballs, often synonymous with pasta, take center stage in the Meatball Bake. This innovative approach transforms the classic duo into a hearty, saucy, and cheesy meal. Ideal for those seeking a lower-carb option without sacrificing flavor, the meatball bake combines the richness of marinara sauce with the gooey goodness of melted mozzarella and parmesan. Adventurous cooks can experiment with alternative sauces, such as a creamy alfredo, to further elevate this comforting dish.

Tuna and White Bean Croquettes with Pesto Dip: Drawing inspiration from the classic Tuscan dish of tuna and white bean salad, chefs are crafting Tuna and White Bean Croquettes. These delightful morsels, crunchy on the outside and creamy within, offer a unique twist suitable for sharing. Paired with a pesto or pesto mayo dip, these croquettes provide a delightful blend of flavors, turning a traditional salad into a shareable and somewhat healthy appetizer.

Ricotta Stuffed Zucchini Rolls:

For those seeking a low-carb alternative to traditional lasagna, Ricotta Stuffed Zucchini Rolls provide a flavorful solution. Sliced zucchini takes the place of pasta sheets, adding a gluten-free dimension to this classic Italian comfort food. In this inventive recipe, Italian sausage contributes richness, although the option to omit it caters to vegetarian preferences, showcasing the adaptability of this modern twist.

The world of modern Italian cuisine is alive with creativity, as chefs and home cooks reimagine classic dishes. From cannoli-inspired chips to polenta fries, meatball bakes, tuna and white bean croquettes, and zucchini lasagna roll-ups, these innovative twists reflect a harmonious blend of tradition and experimentation, inviting everyone to savor the evolving flavors of Italy's culinary heritage.

Chapter 4

Contemporary Italian Cuisine

The evolution of Italian cuisine

The culinary journey of Italian cuisine is a captivating narrative that unfolds across centuries, intricately woven into the fabric of the Roman Empire and the Middle Ages. As Italy itself underwent the ebb and flow of wars, cultural shifts, and global interactions, its cuisine evolved in tandem, becoming a rich tapestry reflecting the nation's dynamic history.

Ancient Roots in Rome:

The origins of Italian cuisine reach deep into the ancestral history of Rome, where feasting was not just a social ritual but a platform for culinary exploration. The Romans, with their political, cultural, and social prowess, reveled in banquets that served as a canvas for the introduction of new and innovative dishes.

Influences from Diverse Cultures:

Italian cuisine, ever adaptive, absorbed influences from diverse cultures and regions. Greek, Arab, and Norman influences left indelible marks, contributing to the culinary mosaic. As far back as the 4th century BC, the cookbook "Apicius" stands as a testament to the culinary sophistication of the time, with the

Romans introducing the use of spices and herbs to enhance flavors.

Renaissance Transformation:

The Renaissance marked a significant chapter in the evolution of Italian cuisine. A culinary renaissance unfolded with the introduction of new ingredients, including tomatoes, potatoes, bell peppers, and maize. This era witnessed a refinement of culinary techniques, a heightened emphasis on presentation, and an infusion of aesthetics into the art of Italian cooking.

World-Renowned Diversity:

Today, Italian cuisine stands as a global culinary ambassador, celebrated for its diversity, simplicity, and commitment to quality. The hallmark of Italian cooking lies in the use of fresh, high-quality ingredients, such as tomatoes, olive oil, garlic, and basil. The enduring popularity of Italian dishes, including pizza, pasta, risotto, and lasagna, attests to the cuisine's universal appeal.

Emphasis on Freshness and Simplicity:

In essence, the story of Italian cuisine is one of resilience and adaptation. It has weathered the tides of time, remaining true to its roots while embracing influences from across the globe. The enduring emphasis on fresh, high-quality ingredients and the pursuit of simple yet delicious flavors define the essence of Italian cooking.

Italian cuisine is not merely a gastronomic tradition; it's a journey through history, culture, and the very essence of Italy itself. Shaped by diverse influences and evolving with the times, it stands as a testament to the resilience of culinary heritage, emphasizing the use of fresh, high-quality ingredients and the art of simplicity that has made it a beloved and enduring global phenomenon.

Max Mariola's contemporary Italian dishes

Spinach and Ricotta Ravioli

Servings: 4

Ingredients:

- 1 package of fresh wonton wrappers
- 1 cup ricotta cheese
- 1 cup fresh spinach, chopped

- 1/2 cup grated Parmesan cheese
- 1 egg
- Salt and pepper to taste
- Olive oil for cooking
- Tomato sauce for serving
- Fresh basil for garnish (optional)

Directions:

Prepare the Filling:

- In a mixing bowl, combine ricotta cheese, chopped fresh spinach, grated Parmesan cheese, and the egg.
- Season the mixture with salt and pepper to taste.
- Mix the ingredients thoroughly until well combined.

Assemble the Ravioli:

- Lay out the wonton wrappers on a clean surface.
- Spoon a small amount of the ricotta and spinach mixture onto the center of each wrapper.
- Moisten the edges of the wrappers with water and fold them over to create a triangle, pressing the edges to seal.

Cook the Ravioli:

- Bring a large pot of salted water to a boil.
- Carefully drop the ravioli into the boiling water and cook for 2-3 minutes or until they float to the surface.
- Remove the ravioli with a slotted spoon and drain.

Serve:

- Heat olive oil in a pan over medium heat.
- Add the cooked ravioli to the pan and sauté briefly until they are lightly browned.
- Serve the ravioli with your favorite tomato sauce.
- Garnish with fresh basil if desired.

Notes:

- This cheat's version uses wonton wrappers instead of making fresh pasta, making it a quick and easy alternative.
- Experiment with different herbs or add a pinch of nutmeg to the filling for extra flavor.

Dan Pepperell's Fried Chicken alla Diavola

Servings: 4

Ingredients:

- 1 whole chicken, cut into pieces

- 2 cups buttermilk
- 2 cups all-purpose flour
- 1 tablespoon paprika
- 1 tablespoon cayenne pepper
- Salt and pepper to taste
- Vegetable oil for frying
- Lemon wedges for serving

Directions:

Marinate the Chicken:

- Place chicken pieces in a large bowl and cover them with buttermilk.
- Let the chicken marinate in the refrigerator for at least 2 hours, or overnight for optimal flavor.

Prepare the Coating:

- In a shallow dish, mix together flour, paprika, cayenne pepper, salt, and pepper.
- Remove chicken pieces from the buttermilk, allowing excess to drip off.

Coat the Chicken:

- Dredge each piece of chicken in the flour mixture, ensuring an even coating.
- Place the coated chicken on a baking sheet and let it rest for 10-15 minutes to set the coating.

Fry the Chicken:

- Heat vegetable oil in a deep fryer or large, deep skillet to 350°F (175°C).
- Carefully lower the chicken pieces into the hot oil and fry until golden brown and cooked through (about 15-20 minutes).

Drain and Serve:

- Remove the fried chicken from the oil and drain on paper towels.
- Sprinkle with additional salt and cayenne pepper if desired.
- Serve the fried chicken hot with lemon wedges on the side.

Notes:

- Adjust the level of cayenne pepper to your spice preference.
- The buttermilk marinade not only adds flavor but also helps tenderize the chicken.
- Serve the fried chicken with a side of coleslaw or pickles for a classic accompaniment.

Capitano's Sugarsnap Pea "Scapece"
Servings: 4

Time Needed: Approximately 40 minutes (including marinating time)

Ingredients:

- 500g sugar snap peas, trimmed
- 1 cup white wine vinegar
- 1 cup water
- 2 cloves garlic, thinly sliced
- Fresh mint leaves
- Salt and pepper to taste
- Extra virgin olive oil for drizzling

Directions:

Blanch the Sugar Snap Peas:

- Bring a large pot of salted water to a boil.
- Add the sugar snap peas and cook for 1-2 minutes until just tender.
- Immediately transfer the peas to an ice bath to stop the cooking process.

Prepare the Marinade:

- In a bowl, mix together white wine vinegar, water, sliced garlic, salt, and pepper.
- Add the blanched sugar snap peas to the marinade and let them sit for at least 30 minutes.

Assemble the Dish:

- Arrange the marinated sugar snap peas on a serving plate.
- Drizzle extra virgin olive oil over the peas.

- Garnish with fresh mint leaves.

Serve:

- Serve the sugarsnap pea "scapece" as a refreshing and tangy appetizer.

Notes:

- This dish can be prepared in advance and refrigerated, allowing the flavors to meld.
- Experiment with different herbs like basil or parsley for added freshness.

Guy Grossi's Pearl Barley Polenta

Servings: 4

Time Needed: Approximately 30 minutes

Ingredients:

- 1 cup pearl barley
- 4 cups chicken or vegetable broth
- 1 cup Parmesan cheese, grated
- 2 tablespoons butter
- Salt and pepper to taste

Directions:

Cook the Pearl Barley:

- Rinse the pearl barley under cold water.

- In a saucepan, bring the broth to a simmer, then add the pearl barley.
- Cook until the barley is tender, stirring occasionally, and adding more broth if needed.

Finish the Polenta:

- Once the barley is cooked, stir in Parmesan cheese and butter.
- Season with salt and pepper to taste.

Serve:

- Spoon the pearl barley polenta onto plates or into bowls.

Notes:

- Pearl barley adds a nutty flavor and chewy texture to the polenta.
- Adjust the consistency by adding more broth if you prefer a creamier polenta.

Acme's Maltagliati with Washed Kimchi and Guanciale

Servings: 4

Time Needed: Approximately 40 minutes

Ingredients:

- 400g maltagliati pasta (or any preferred pasta)
- 200g guanciale, thinly sliced

- 1 cup washed kimchi, chopped
- 2 cloves garlic, minced
- 1/4 cup extra virgin olive oil
- Salt and pepper to taste
- Fresh parsley for garnish

Directions:

Cook the Pasta:

- Cook the maltagliati pasta in salted boiling water until al dente.
- Reserve a cup of pasta cooking water before draining.

Sauté Guanciale and Garlic:

- In a large pan, heat olive oil over medium heat.
- Add guanciale slices and cook until they become crispy.
- Add minced garlic and sauté until fragrant.

Combine with Kimchi:

- Add chopped washed kimchi to the pan and toss to combine.
- Cook for a few minutes until the kimchi is heated through.

Combine with Pasta:

- Add the cooked maltagliati pasta to the pan, tossing to coat the pasta in the flavorful mixture.
- If needed, add a bit of the reserved pasta cooking water to achieve the desired consistency.

Serve:

- Garnish with fresh parsley and serve immediately.

Notes:

- Maltagliati, meaning "badly cut," is a type of Italian pasta that adds a rustic touch to the dish.
- Adjust the level of spiciness by controlling the amount of kimchi.

Pinbone's Hazelnut Tiramisù

Servings: 6

Time Needed: Approximately 30 minutes (plus chilling time)

Ingredients:

- 4 large egg yolks
- 1 cup sugar
- 1 cup mascarpone cheese
- 1 cup heavy cream

- 1 cup brewed espresso, cooled
- 1/2 cup hazelnut liqueur
- 1 cup hazelnuts, toasted and chopped
- Ladyfinger biscuits

Directions:

Prepare the Egg Mixture:

- In a bowl, whisk together egg yolks and sugar until the mixture becomes pale and creamy.
- Add mascarpone cheese and continue to whisk until well combined.

Whip the Cream:

- In a separate bowl, whip the heavy cream until stiff peaks form.
- Gently fold the whipped cream into the egg and mascarpone mixture.

Prepare the Espresso Mixture:

- Combine brewed espresso and hazelnut liqueur in a shallow dish.

Assemble the Tiramisù:

- Dip each ladyfinger into the espresso mixture and layer them at the bottom of serving glasses or a dish.
- Spoon a layer of the egg and mascarpone mixture over the ladyfingers.
- Sprinkle a layer of chopped hazelnuts.

Repeat Layers:

- Repeat the layers until you reach the top of the serving dish.
- Finish with a layer of hazelnuts on top.

Chill and Serve:

- Refrigerate the tiramisù for at least 4 hours or overnight to allow flavors to meld.

Serve chilled.

Notes:

- Customize the level of hazelnut flavor by adjusting the amount of hazelnut liqueur.
- This hazelnut tiramisù offers a unique twist to the traditional recipe.

Parmesan Chawanmushi

Servings: 4

Time Needed: Approximately 30 minutes

Ingredients:

4 large eggs

- 2 cups dashi (Japanese soup stock)
- 1/2 cup heavy cream
- 1/2 cup Parmesan cheese, grated
- 1/2 cup shiitake mushrooms, sliced
- 1/2 cup cooked chicken, shredded

- 1/4 cup green onions, finely chopped
- Salt and white pepper to taste

Directions:

Prepare Chawanmushi Base:

- In a bowl, beat the eggs and then add dashi, heavy cream, Parmesan cheese, salt, and white pepper. Mix well.

Prepare Individual Servings:

- Distribute shiitake mushrooms, cooked chicken, and green onions evenly among individual chawanmushi cups or small heatproof bowls.

Pour Egg Mixture:

- Pour the egg mixture into each cup, covering the ingredients.

Steam:

- Place the cups in a steamer or a deep pan with a lid.
- Steam for about 15-20 minutes or until the chawanmushi is set.

Serve:

- Serve the Parmesan chawanmushi hot, garnished with additional green onions if desired.

Notes:

- Chawanmushi is a Japanese steamed egg custard, and this version incorporates Italian Parmesan for a fusion twist.
- Experiment with other ingredients like seafood or vegetables based on preference.

Carpaccio of Kangaroo with Beetroot and Native Fruits

Servings: 2

Time Needed: Approximately 15 minutes

Ingredients:

- 200g kangaroo fillet, thinly sliced
- 1 medium-sized beetroot, peeled and thinly sliced
- Assorted native fruits (such as finger limes, bush tomatoes)
- Olive oil
- Salt and pepper to taste
- Microgreens for garnish

Directions:

Prepare Kangaroo Carpaccio:

- Lay out the thinly sliced kangaroo fillet on a serving plate.

Arrange Beetroot and Native Fruits:

- Artfully arrange the beetroot slices and assorted native fruits over the kangaroo.

Drizzle with Olive Oil:

- Drizzle the dish with high-quality olive oil.

Season:

- Season with salt and pepper to taste.

Garnish:

- Garnish the carpaccio with microgreens for a fresh touch.

Serve:

- Serve immediately as an elegant appetizer or light main course.

Notes:

- Kangaroo meat is lean and flavorful, and when prepared as carpaccio, it offers a unique and exotic dining experience.
- Experiment with different native fruits for a varied and vibrant dish.

Swordfish con Sarde

Servings: 4

Time Needed: Approximately 30 minutes

Ingredients:

- 4 swordfish fillets
- 8 fresh sardines, cleaned and gutted
- 1 cup fresh breadcrumbs
- 1/2 cup pine nuts
- 1/2 cup currants
- 4 cloves garlic, minced
- Fresh parsley, chopped
- Olive oil
- Salt and pepper to taste
- Lemon wedges for serving

Directions:

Prepare Swordfish Fillets:

- Season swordfish fillets with salt, pepper, and a drizzle of olive oil.

Prepare Sardines:

- Season cleaned sardines with salt and pepper.

Make Stuffing:

- In a bowl, combine fresh breadcrumbs, pine nuts, currants, minced garlic, and chopped fresh parsley.

Stuff Swordfish and Sardines:

- Stuff each swordfish fillet with the breadcrumb mixture and place two sardines on top.
- Secure with toothpicks.

Grill or Pan-Sear:

- Grill or pan-sear the swordfish and sardines until cooked through.

Serve:

- Remove toothpicks before serving.
- Drizzle with olive oil and serve with lemon wedges.

Notes:

- This dish, known as "Swordfish con Sarde," combines the richness of swordfish with the flavors of fresh sardines for a delightful seafood experience.
- Adjust stuffing ingredients to personal preference.

Popolo's Frittata "Carbonara"

Servings: 4-6

Time Needed: Approximately 25 minutes

Ingredients:

- 8 large eggs
- 1/2 cup grated Pecorino Romano cheese
- 1/2 cup grated Parmesan cheese
- 200g pancetta, diced
- 1 onion, finely chopped
- 1 cup frozen peas, thawed
- Salt and pepper to taste
- Fresh chives, chopped, for garnish

Directions:

Prepare Pancetta and Onion:

- In an ovenproof skillet, cook diced pancetta until crispy. Add finely chopped onion and cook until softened.

Whisk Eggs and Cheese:

- In a bowl, whisk together eggs, Pecorino Romano, and Parmesan cheese.

Combine Ingredients:

- Add the thawed peas to the skillet with the pancetta and onion.

- Pour the egg and cheese mixture over the ingredients in the skillet.

Cook on Stovetop:

- Cook on the stovetop over medium heat until the edges set.

Finish in the Oven:

- Transfer the skillet to a preheated oven and broil until the top is golden brown and the frittata is set.

Garnish and Serve:

- Garnish with chopped fresh chives and serve.

Notes:

- This frittata takes inspiration from the classic Roman pasta dish "Carbonara," incorporating pancetta, cheese, and peas.
- Ensure the skillet is ovenproof for a seamless transition from stovetop to oven.

Max Mariola favorite contemporary Italian dishes

Smoked Eel Carbonara

Servings: 2-3

Time Needed: Approximately 30 minutes

Ingredients:

- 250g smoked eel, sliced
- 400g wonton wrappers
- 4 egg yolks
- 1 cup grated Pecorino Romano cheese
- 1 cup grated Parmesan cheese
- Freshly ground black pepper
- Olive oil
- Fresh parsley, chopped (for garnish)

Directions:

Prepare Wonton Wrappers:

- Cut wonton wrappers into thin strips resembling traditional pasta.

Cook Wonton "Pasta":

- Boil the wonton strips until al dente, then drain and set aside.

Make Carbonara Sauce:

- In a bowl, whisk together egg yolks, Pecorino Romano, Parmesan, and black pepper to create a creamy sauce.

Sauté Smoked Eel:

In a pan, sauté sliced smoked eel in olive oil until slightly crispy.

Combine Ingredients:

- Toss the cooked wonton "pasta" with the carbonara sauce, ensuring an even coating.
- Add the sautéed smoked eel and mix gently.

Serve:

- Plate the smoked eel carbonara, garnish with fresh parsley, and grind additional black pepper if desired.

Notes:

- The wonton wrappers add a unique texture to the dish, and the smoked eel provides a smoky, savory flavor.
- This recipe offers a playful twist on the traditional carbonara.

Pici Bolognese with Fish Sauce

Servings: 4-5

Time Needed: Approximately 45 minutes

Ingredients:

- 400g pici pasta
- 500g ground beef
- 1 onion, finely chopped
- 2 cloves garlic, minced
- 1 cup tomato sauce
- 2 tbsp fish sauce
- Salt and pepper to taste
- Olive oil
- Grated Parmesan cheese (for serving)

Directions:

Cook Pici Pasta:

- Boil pici pasta in salted water until al dente. Drain and set aside.

Prepare Bolognese Sauce:

- In a pan, sauté onions and garlic in olive oil until softened.
- Add ground beef and cook until browned. Drain excess fat.

Add Sauces:

- Pour in tomato sauce and fish sauce. Simmer until the sauce thickens. Season with salt and pepper.

Combine with Pici:

- Toss the cooked pici pasta into the Bolognese sauce, ensuring it's well-coated.

Serve:

- Plate the dish and sprinkle with grated Parmesan cheese.

Notes:

- The addition of fish sauce brings a depth of umami flavor to the traditional Bolognese.
- Pici pasta's thickness complements the hearty sauce.

Roasted Crispy Broccoli with Parmigiano Reggiano and Garlic

Servings: 4

Time Needed: Approximately 20 minutes

Ingredients:

- 500g broccoli florets
- 3 tbsp olive oil
- 4 garlic cloves, minced

- 1/2 cup Parmigiano Reggiano, grated
- Salt and black pepper to taste
- Red pepper flakes (optional)
- Lemon wedges (for serving)

Directions:

Roast Broccoli:

- Preheat the oven to 220°C. Toss broccoli with olive oil, minced garlic, salt, and pepper. Roast until crispy and golden.

Add Cheese:

- Sprinkle grated Parmigiano Reggiano over the roasted broccoli. Return to the oven for a few minutes until the cheese melts.

Serve:

- Transfer the broccoli to a serving dish. Optionally, sprinkle red pepper flakes for extra heat. Serve with lemon wedges.

Notes:

- Roasting enhances the broccoli's natural sweetness, and Parmigiano Reggiano adds a rich, savory flavor.
- This appetizer is quick, easy, and a crowd-pleaser.

Burrata and Tomato Salad

Servings: 4

Time Needed: Approximately 15 minutes

Ingredients:

- 2 large burrata balls
- 4 large heirloom tomatoes, sliced
- Fresh basil leaves
- Extra virgin olive oil
- Balsamic glaze (optional)
- Salt and black pepper to taste

Directions:

Prepare Burrata:

- Cut burrata balls into halves or quarters, depending on preference.

Assemble Salad:

- Arrange sliced heirloom tomatoes on a serving platter. Place burrata pieces on top.

Garnish:

- Scatter fresh basil leaves over the salad. Drizzle with olive oil and balsamic glaze if desired.

Season:

- Sprinkle salt and black pepper over the salad.

Notes:

- Burrata adds a creamy texture to the salad, complementing the sweetness of heirloom tomatoes.
- A simple yet elegant dish, perfect as an appetizer or light lunch.

Pork Milanese with Arugula Salad

Servings: 4

Time Needed: Approximately 30 minutes

Ingredients:

- 4 pork cutlets
- 1 cup breadcrumbs
- 2 eggs, beaten
- 1 cup all-purpose flour
- 1/2 cup Parmesan cheese, grated
- Salt and black pepper to taste
- 4 cups arugula
- Cherry tomatoes, halved
- Lemon wedges
- Olive oil for frying

Directions:

Prepare Breading Station:

- Set up three shallow dishes with flour, beaten eggs, and a mixture of breadcrumbs and grated Parmesan.

Bread Pork Cutlets:

- Season pork cutlets with salt and pepper. Dredge in flour, dip in beaten eggs, then coat with breadcrumb mixture.

Fry Cutlets:

- Heat olive oil in a pan over medium-high heat. Fry breaded cutlets until golden brown and cooked through.

Assemble Salad:

- Toss arugula and cherry tomatoes in a bowl. Dress with olive oil, salt, and pepper.

Serve:

- Place pork cutlets on a plate, top with arugula salad. Serve with lemon wedges.

Notes:

- The arugula salad provides a refreshing contrast to the crispy pork cutlets.

- A modern twist on the classic Milanese, combining textures and flavors.

Chapter 5

Pasta and Risotto

Importance of pasta and risotto in Italian cuisine.

Pasta and risotto, woven into the fabric of Italian culinary heritage, stand as timeless pillars in the gastronomic journey of this vibrant culture. These dishes, adorned with simplicity and versatility, have graced Italian tables for centuries, earning a cherished place in the hearts of both locals and global admirers.

Pasta: A Culinary Emblem

Pasta, an emblematic symbol of Italian gastronomy, has entrenched itself in the culinary DNA of the nation. Its origins are as rich and diverse as the sauces it generously embraces. Often regarded as a comfort food, pasta's allure lies in its ability to transform ordinary ingredients into extraordinary meals.

Picture a bustling Italian kitchen, the air filled with the harmonious symphony of simmering sauces and the comforting aroma of pasta boiling to perfection. Pasta offers a canvas for creativity, accommodating an array of sauces, from the robust ragù to the simplicity of aglio e olio.

Versatility is pasta's forte, gracing the table as a swift and satisfying meal. Whether drenched in a hearty

Bolognese or adorned with a light olive oil drizzle and fresh herbs, pasta adapts to diverse tastes and occasions, embodying the essence of Italian familial gatherings.

Risotto: The Art of Creamy Elegance

Venture into the realm of primo piatto, and you'll encounter the exquisite dance of rice in the form of risotto. Born from an ancient relationship with Asia, rice found its way into Italian fields, becoming a staple crop in the North. Risotto, crafted from special Italian rice varieties, emerges as a culinary masterpiece.

Enter an Italian kitchen, and the symphony of risotto begins. The velvety texture, the nuanced flavors – risotto is a celebration of simplicity and sophistication. The cultivation of rice, particularly in the North, has elevated risotto to a regional delicacy, with each grain absorbing the essence of the dish.

Asparagus, mushrooms, cheese – these are the artisans that collaborate with the rice to produce a dish that is as comforting as it is refined. Risotto mirrors the changing seasons, with variations that echo the bounties of the land. It is a canvas for culinary expression, a creamy testament to the artistry embedded in Italian cooking.

Pasta and Risotto Epitomize Italian cuisine's spirit – a harmony of tradition, simplicity, and adaptability. Whether in the cozy kitchen of a rustic trattoria or the bustling quarters of a modern household, these dishes transcend time, uniting generations in the shared joy of a well-prepared meal. From the savoriness of pasta to the creamy elegance of risotto, the culinary symphony of Italy continues to captivate palates around the world.

Max Mariola's favorite pasta and risotto dishes.

Spaghetti with Clams and Mussels

Servings: 4

Time Needed: Approximately 25 minutes

Ingredients:

- 400g spaghetti
- 500g fresh clams, scrubbed
- 500g fresh mussels, cleaned and debearded
- 4 cloves garlic, minced
- 1/2 cup fresh parsley, chopped
- 1 cup dry white wine
- 1/4 cup olive oil
- Salt and black pepper to taste
- Red pepper flakes (optional)

Directions:

Prepare Seafood:

- Rinse clams and mussels thoroughly. Discard any open or damaged ones.

Sauté Aromatics:

- In a large pan, heat olive oil over medium heat. Add minced garlic and sauté until fragrant.

Cook Seafood:

- Add clams and mussels to the pan. Pour in white wine, cover, and cook until shells open (discard any unopened shells).

Cook Spaghetti:

- Meanwhile, cook spaghetti in salted boiling water until al dente. Drain.

Combine and Serve:

- Toss cooked spaghetti with the seafood, garlic, and wine sauce. Season with salt, black pepper, and red pepper flakes if desired. Garnish with fresh parsley.

Notes:

- Ensure all clams and mussels are fresh and alive before cooking.
- The white wine sauce adds depth to the seafood flavors.

Saffron Spaghetti Cooked Risotto-Style

Servings: 3-4

Time Needed: Approximately 30 minutes

Ingredients:

- 300g saffron-infused spaghetti
- 1 cup Arborio rice
- 1/2 cup dry white wine
- 4 cups chicken or vegetable broth, kept warm
- 1 small onion, finely chopped
- 2 tbsp olive oil
- 1/2 cup Parmesan cheese, grated
- Salt and pepper to taste
- Fresh parsley, chopped (for garnish)

Directions:

Sauté Onion:

- In a large pan, heat olive oil over medium heat. Sauté chopped onion until translucent.

Cook Arborio Rice:

- Add Arborio rice to the pan and toast it for a couple of minutes until it becomes slightly translucent.

Deglaze with Wine:

- Pour in the white wine, stirring continuously until it's mostly absorbed.

Add Broth:

- Begin adding warm broth one ladle at a time, stirring frequently. Allow the liquid to be absorbed before adding more.

Cook Spaghetti Risotto-Style:

- Once the rice is almost cooked, add saffron-infused spaghetti to the pan. Continue adding broth and stirring until the spaghetti is al dente.

Finish and Serve:

- Stir in Parmesan cheese, salt, and pepper. Garnish with fresh parsley.

Notes:

- Cooking spaghetti risotto-style infuses the dish with a creamy texture and allows the saffron flavor to permeate each strand.
- This method requires attention but results in a unique and flavorful dish.

Pesto Risotto with Roasted Tomatoes

Servings: 4-5

Time Needed: Approximately 35 minutes

Ingredients:

- 1 1/2 cups Arborio rice
- 1/2 cup dry white wine
- 4 cups chicken or vegetable broth, kept warm
- 1 cup cherry tomatoes, halved
- 1/2 cup basil pesto
- 1/2 cup Parmesan cheese, grated
- 1 small onion, finely chopped
- 2 tbsp olive oil
- Salt and black pepper to taste
- Pine nuts (for garnish)

Directions:

Roast Tomatoes:

- Preheat the oven to 200°C. Toss cherry tomatoes with olive oil, salt, and pepper. Roast until slightly caramelized.

Sauté Onion:

- In a large pan, sauté chopped onion in olive oil until softened.

Cook Arborio Rice:

- Add Arborio rice to the pan and toast it for a couple of minutes until it becomes slightly translucent.

Deglaze with Wine:

- Pour in the white wine, stirring continuously until it's mostly absorbed.

Add Broth:

- Begin adding warm broth one ladle at a time, stirring frequently.

Combine Pesto and Tomatoes:

- Once the rice is almost cooked, stir in basil pesto and roasted cherry tomatoes.

Finish and Serve:

- Stir in Parmesan cheese until creamy. Garnish with pine nuts.

Notes:

- Pesto adds a burst of fresh herbaceous flavor, and roasted tomatoes bring sweetness and acidity.
- This dish marries the vibrant flavors of pesto with the creamy texture of risotto.

Risotto with Asparagus and Crescenza Cheese

Servings: 4

Time Needed: 30 minutes

Ingredients:

- 1 ½ cups Arborio rice
- 1 bunch asparagus, trimmed and chopped
- 1 small onion, finely chopped

- 2 cloves garlic, minced
- 4 cups chicken or vegetable broth, kept warm
- 1 cup dry white wine
- ½ cup Crescenza cheese, diced
- 1/3 cup Parmesan cheese, grated
- 2 tablespoons olive oil
- Salt and pepper to taste
- Fresh parsley, chopped (for garnish)

Directions:

- In a large pan, heat olive oil over medium heat. Add onions and garlic, sauté until softened.
- Add Arborio rice, stirring to coat each grain with oil, until slightly toasted.
- Pour in the white wine, allowing it to be absorbed by the rice.
- Begin adding warm broth, one ladle at a time, stirring frequently. Wait until each addition is mostly absorbed before adding more.
- After about 10 minutes, add chopped asparagus to the risotto.
- Continue the process until the rice is creamy and cooked to al dente, usually around 18-20 minutes.
- Stir in Crescenza and Parmesan cheese, ensuring a creamy consistency.
- Season with salt and pepper to taste.
- Garnish with fresh parsley and serve immediately.

Notes: This risotto is best enjoyed promptly to relish its creamy texture.

Pasta with Cime di Rapa and Totani

Servings: 3-4

Time Needed: 25 minutes

Ingredients:

- 12 oz pasta of your choice
- 1 bunch cime di rapa (broccoli rabe), trimmed
- 2 small totani (squid), cleaned and sliced
- 3 cloves garlic, sliced
- 1 teaspoon red pepper flakes
- ¼ cup extra-virgin olive oil
- Salt to taste
- Grated Pecorino Romano cheese (for serving)

Directions:

- Cook the pasta in salted boiling water until al dente.
- Blanch cime di rapa in the pasta water for 3 minutes. Drain and set aside.
- In a pan, heat olive oil over medium heat. Add garlic and red pepper flakes.
- Add sliced totani to the pan, cooking until they turn opaque.
- Toss in blanched cime di rapa, sauté for an additional 2-3 minutes.

- Mix in the cooked pasta, ensuring it's well-coated with the sauce.
- Season with salt to taste.
- Serve hot, topped with Pecorino Romano cheese.

Notes: Adjust the red pepper flakes according to your spice preference.

Pasta with Fungi Cardoncelli and Salsiccia

Servings: 4

Time Needed: 40 minutes

Ingredients:

- 14 oz pasta
- 1 lb cardoncelli mushrooms, sliced
- 1 lb Italian salsiccia (sausage), casing removed
- 1 onion, finely chopped
- 2 cloves garlic, minced
- ½ cup dry white wine
- 1 cup heavy cream
- 2 tablespoons olive oil
- Salt and pepper to taste
- Fresh parsley, chopped (for garnish)

Directions:

- Cook the pasta in salted boiling water until al dente.
- In a pan, heat olive oil over medium heat. Add onions and garlic, sauté until softened.
- Add sliced cardoncelli mushrooms, cooking until they release their moisture.
- Crumble in the salsiccia, cooking until browned.
- Pour in the white wine, allowing it to reduce.
- Add heavy cream, stirring to create a luscious sauce.
- Mix in the cooked pasta, ensuring it's well-coated.
- Season with salt and pepper to taste.
- Garnish with fresh parsley and serve hot.

Notes: A delightful indulgence, this pasta is a celebration of hearty flavors.

Chapter 6

Seafood

Importance of seafood in Italian cuisine
Seafood holds a paramount position in Italian cuisine, playing a pivotal role in shaping the country's culinary identity. The importance of seafood in Italian gastronomy is deeply rooted in its geographical characteristics, with Italy being surrounded by the Mediterranean Sea on three sides. This natural abundance of marine resources has significantly influenced the culinary traditions of various regions, offering a diverse array of fresh and flavorful ingredients.

One key aspect of seafood's importance in Italian cuisine is its role in promoting a healthy and balanced diet. Rich in omega-3 fatty acids, vitamins, and minerals, seafood aligns with the Mediterranean diet, which is renowned for its numerous health benefits. Italians have long recognized the nutritional value of seafood, incorporating it into their meals as a source of lean protein and essential nutrients.

Beyond its nutritional significance, seafood represents a celebration of regional diversity in Italian cooking. Coastal regions showcase an array of distinct seafood dishes, reflecting local preferences and the unique offerings of the surrounding seas.

From Sicily's renowned swordfish dishes to the Ligurian coast's focus on anchovies and seafood-laden pasta, each region contributes its own distinct flavors to the broader tapestry of Italian seafood cuisine.

Furthermore, the cultural and social aspects of seafood in Italy cannot be overstated. Seafood meals are often associated with communal gatherings, festive occasions, and family traditions. The act of sharing a seafood feast symbolizes conviviality and togetherness, highlighting the social importance of these dishes.

Italian chefs, known for their commitment to using fresh, high-quality ingredients, emphasize the role of seafood in elevating the culinary experience. From iconic dishes like Risotto ai Frutti di Mare (seafood risotto) to simpler preparations like grilled fish dressed in olive oil and herbs, Italian seafood recipes showcase a mastery of both technique and respect for the natural flavors of the ingredients.

The importance of seafood in Italian cuisine extends far beyond mere sustenance. It is an integral part of the country's gastronomic heritage, representing a harmonious blend of health, regional diversity, and social connections, all contributing to the rich tapestry of Italian culinary traditions.

Max Mariola's favorite seafood dishes

Linguine allo Scoglio

Servings: 4
Time Needed: 30 minutes

Ingredients:

- 400g linguine
- 500g mixed seafood (shrimp, mussels, clams, squid), fresh and local if possible
- 4 cloves garlic, minced
- 1 teaspoon red pepper flakes
- 1 cup cherry tomatoes, halved
- 1/2 cup white wine
- Fresh parsley, chopped
- Salt and pepper to taste
- Olive oil

Directions:

- Cook linguine al dente according to package instructions.
- In a large pan, heat olive oil over medium heat. Add minced garlic and red pepper flakes, sauté until fragrant.
- Add mixed seafood to the pan, cooking until they start to turn opaque.
- Pour in white wine and let it simmer for a couple of minutes.

- Toss in halved cherry tomatoes and cook until they soften.
- Season with salt and pepper, then add cooked linguine to the pan.
- Mix everything together, ensuring the pasta is coated with the flavorful sauce.
- Garnish with fresh parsley and serve immediately.

Notes: This dish thrives on the freshness of the seafood, so try to source local, fresh catches for an authentic taste.

Fritto Misto di Pesce

Servings: 4

Time Needed: 20 minutes

Ingredients:

- 500g assorted seafood (shrimp, squid, small fish)
- 1 cup all-purpose flour
- Salt and pepper to taste
- Vegetable oil for frying
- Lemon wedges for serving

Directions:

- In a bowl, mix flour, salt, and pepper.

- Coat the seafood in the flour mixture, shaking off excess.
- Heat vegetable oil in a deep pan to 350°F.
- Fry the seafood in batches until golden brown and crispy.
- Drain on paper towels and sprinkle with salt.
- Serve immediately with lemon wedges.

Notes: Fritto Misto is best enjoyed hot and crispy. Ensure the oil is at the right temperature for perfect frying.

Spaghetti alle Vongole

Servings: 4

Time Needed: 25 minutes

Ingredients:

- 400g spaghetti
- 1kg fresh clams, cleaned
- 4 cloves garlic, thinly sliced
- 1/2 teaspoon red pepper flakes
- 1/2 cup white wine
- Fresh parsley, chopped
- Olive oil
- Salt and pepper to taste

Directions:

- Cook spaghetti al dente according to package instructions.
- In a large pan, sauté garlic and red pepper flakes in olive oil until garlic is golden.
- Add cleaned clams to the pan, pour in white wine, and cover until clams open.
- Toss in cooked spaghetti, ensuring it's coated in the clam-infused sauce.
- Season with salt and pepper, garnish with fresh parsley, and serve immediately.

Notes: Use only fresh and closed clams. Discard any that don't open after cooking.

Linguine all'Astice:

Servings: 4

Time Needed: 40 minutes

Directions:

- 400g linguine
- 2 lobsters, cooked and meat removed
- 4 cloves garlic, minced
- 1/2 teaspoon red pepper flakes
- 1 cup cherry tomatoes, halved
- 1/2 cup tomato sauce
- Fresh basil, chopped
- Salt and pepper to taste

- Olive oil

Directions:

- Cook linguine al dente according to package instructions.
- In a pan, sauté minced garlic and red pepper flakes in olive oil until fragrant.
- Add lobster meat and halved cherry tomatoes, cooking until tomatoes soften.
- Pour in tomato sauce, season with salt and pepper, and let it simmer.
- Toss in cooked linguine, ensuring it's coated in the lobster-infused sauce.
- Garnish with fresh basil and serve immediately.

Notes: Use pre-cooked lobster for convenience. Adjust the spice level by controlling the red pepper flakes.

Risotto ai Frutti di Mare

Servings: 4

Time Needed: 30 minutes

Ingredients:

- 1 cup Arborio rice
- 500g mixed seafood (shrimp, mussels, clams)
- 4 cups fish or seafood broth

- 1/2 cup white wine
- 1 onion, finely chopped
- 2 cloves garlic, minced
- Fresh parsley, chopped
- Olive oil
- Salt and pepper to taste
- Parmesan cheese for serving

Directions:

- In a pan, sauté chopped onion and minced garlic in olive oil until translucent.
- Add Arborio rice, toasting it until it's lightly golden.
- Pour in white wine, allowing it to be absorbed by the rice.
- Begin adding fish or seafood broth, one ladle at a time, allowing each addition to be absorbed before adding the next.
- Stir continuously to achieve a creamy consistency. Continue until the rice is al dente.
- In a separate pan, cook mixed seafood until done.
- Fold the cooked seafood into the risotto, garnish with fresh parsley, and season with salt and pepper.
- Serve hot with grated Parmesan cheese.

Chapter 7

Meat and Poultry

Importance of meat and poultry in Italian cuisine

Meat and poultry play a pivotal role in Italian cuisine, contributing to the rich and diverse tapestry of flavors that define this culinary tradition. Italy, with its various regions and local specialties, showcases a profound appreciation for high-quality, locally sourced meats. Here's an exploration of the importance of meat and poultry in Italian cuisine:

Regional Diversity:

Italian cuisine is renowned for its regional diversity, and this is prominently reflected in meat and poultry dishes. Different regions boast their unique meat specialties, such as Bistecca alla Fiorentina from Tuscany, Osso Buco from Lombardy, or Sicilian-style Salsiccia.

Staple Ingredients:

Meat, particularly pork, beef, and lamb, serves as a staple ingredient in many traditional Italian recipes. It is often used to create hearty and comforting dishes that are central to Italian home-cooking, reflecting a deep connection to local agriculture and husbandry.

Art of Slow Cooking:

Italian cuisine places a strong emphasis on slow cooking techniques, allowing meats to simmer and marinate in flavorful sauces. This method enhances the tenderness and taste of the meat. Dishes like Ragu Bolognese and Ossobuco are testament to the Italian commitment to slow-cooked perfection.

Versatility of Poultry:

Poultry, especially chicken and duck, is highly valued in Italian kitchens for its versatility. From the simplicity of Chicken Cacciatore to the sophistication of Duck Risotto, poultry adapts to various regional styles, showcasing the culinary diversity across the country.

Celebration of Festivals and Traditions:

Meat and poultry take center stage during festive occasions and cultural traditions. Roast meats, such as porchetta or roast lamb, are often featured during celebratory feasts, symbolizing abundance and togetherness.

Charcuterie and Cured Meats:

Italian charcuterie is globally celebrated, with a vast array of cured meats like prosciutto, salami, and bresaola. These cured meats are not only enjoyed on their own but also play a crucial role in antipasti platters and as ingredients in many pasta and risotto dishes.

Farm-to-Table Philosophy:

Italy's farm-to-table philosophy is evident in the emphasis on locally sourced, high-quality meats. Whether it's the famed Chianina beef or free-range poultry, Italians prioritize the freshness and origin of their meat, contributing to the authenticity of their cuisine.

Integration into Pasta and Risotto:

Meat and poultry seamlessly integrate into pasta and risotto dishes, adding depth and heartiness. From the classic Bolognese sauce to the innovative Duck and Porcini Risotto, these dishes showcase the adaptability of meat in Italian culinary creativity.

Family and Social Bonds:

Sharing a meal, often centered around meat dishes, is a fundamental aspect of Italian culture. The preparation and enjoyment of meat-based meals strengthen family bonds, fostering a sense of community and togetherness.

Meat and poultry in Italian cuisine extend beyond mere sustenance; they are integral components of a culinary heritage deeply rooted in tradition, regional diversity, and a profound respect for the finest ingredients. From the simplicity of a Tuscan steak to the complexity of a Milanese Osso Buco, these meat-centric dishes are a testament to the enduring legacy of Italian gastronomy.

Max Mariola's favorite meat and poultry dishes

Osso Buco

Servings: 4

Ingredients:

- 4 veal shanks
- 1 onion, chopped
- 2 cloves garlic, minced
- 2 carrots, chopped
- 2 celery stalks, chopped
- 400g canned tomatoes
- 1 cup beef broth
- 1/2 cup white wine
- 2 tbsp olive oil
- 2 tbsp butter
- 1 lemon, zested
- Salt and pepper

Directions:

- Preheat the oven to 180°C.
- In a pan, heat the olive oil and butter over medium heat. Add the onion, garlic, carrots, and celery. Cook until softened.

- Add the veal shanks and brown on all sides.
- Add the canned tomatoes, beef broth, white wine, lemon zest, salt, and pepper. Bring to a boil.
- Transfer the mixture to an oven-safe dish and cover with foil.
- Bake in the oven for 2-3 hours, or until the meat is tender.
- Serve hot.

Pollo alla Cacciatora

Servings: 4

Ingredients:

- 4 chicken thighs
- 1 onion, chopped
- 2 cloves garlic, minced
- 400g canned tomatoes
- 1/2 cup chicken broth
- 1/2 cup white wine
- 1 tbsp capers
- 1 tbsp black olives, pitted
- 1 tbsp fresh rosemary, chopped
- Salt and pepper
- Olive oil

Directions:

- Preheat the oven to 180°C.

- In a pan, heat some olive oil over medium heat. Add the chicken thighs and brown on all sides.
- Remove the chicken from the pan and set aside.
- In the same pan, add the onion and garlic. Cook until softened.
- Add the canned tomatoes, chicken broth, white wine, capers, olives, rosemary, salt, and pepper. Bring to a boil.
- Return the chicken to the pan and cover with the tomato sauce.
- Transfer the mixture to an oven-safe dish and bake in the oven for 30-40 minutes, or until the chicken is cooked through.
- Serve hot.

Bistecca alla Fiorentina

Servings: 2-4

Time Needed: 30 minutes (plus additional time for marination)

Ingredients:

- 1 large T-bone or Porterhouse steak (about 2 inches thick)
- Coarse salt (preferably sea salt)
- Freshly ground black pepper
- Extra virgin olive oil

Directions:

- Prepare the Steak: Take the steak out of the refrigerator and let it come to room temperature for about 30 minutes. This ensures even cooking.
- Season the Steak: Generously season the steak on both sides with coarse salt. Be liberal, as this contributes to the crust formation during cooking. Allow it to sit for another 15 minutes.
- Preheat the Grill or Pan: Heat your grill or a cast-iron pan to high heat. It should be smoking hot.
- Cook the Steak: Place the steak on the hot grill or pan. Cook for about 5-7 minutes on each side for a medium-rare doneness. Adjust the time based on your preferred level of doneness.
- Rest the Steak: Once cooked, remove the steak from the heat and let it rest for 10 minutes. This allows the juices to redistribute, keeping the steak moist.
- Slice and Serve: Slice the steak against the grain into thick slices. Drizzle extra virgin olive oil over the top. Serve immediately.

Notes: Bistecca alla Fiorentina is traditionally served rare to medium-rare. Make sure to use a high-quality steak, preferably from the Chianina breed for an authentic experience.

Porchetta

Servings: 8-10

Time Needed: 3-4 hours (plus overnight marination)

Ingredients:

- 5-6 lb pork belly, skin on
- 2 tablespoons fennel seeds
- 4 cloves garlic, minced
- 1 tablespoon fresh rosemary, chopped
- Zest of 1 lemon
- Salt and black pepper
- Olive oil

Directions:

- Prepare the Pork Belly: Score the skin of the pork belly in a crosshatch pattern. Rub salt on the skin and let it sit in the refrigerator overnight.
- Preheat the Oven: Preheat the oven to 300°F (150°C).
- Make the Filling: In a mortar, crush the fennel seeds. Mix them with minced garlic, rosemary, lemon zest, salt, and pepper.
- Season and Roll: Pat the pork belly dry. Rub the filling mixture over the meat side. Roll the pork belly tightly and tie it with kitchen twine.
- Roast: Rub the skin with olive oil and additional salt. Roast the porchetta in the

preheated oven for about 3-4 hours or until the internal temperature reaches 160°F (70°C).
- Crisp the Skin: For the last 30 minutes, increase the oven temperature to 475°F (245°C) to crisp up the skin.
- Rest and Serve: Let the porchetta rest for at least 20 minutes before slicing. Serve in slices or sandwiches.

Notes: Porchetta is a festive dish often served during celebrations. The crispy skin is a highlight, so ensure it gets the high heat treatment for the perfect crackling.

Arrosto di Maiale (Italian Roast Pork)

Servings: 6-8

Time Needed: 2.5-3 hours

Direction:

- 3-4 lb pork loin roast
- 4 cloves garlic, sliced
- 2 tablespoons fresh rosemary, chopped
- 1 tablespoon fresh sage, chopped
- Salt and black pepper
- Olive oil

Directions:

- Preheat the Oven: Preheat the oven to 350°F (175°C).
- Prepare the Roast: Make small incisions in the pork loin and insert slices of garlic.
- Season: Rub the pork with salt, pepper, rosemary, and sage. Drizzle with olive oil.
- Sear the Roast: In an oven-safe pan, sear the pork on all sides over medium-high heat until browned.
- Roast in the Oven: Place the pan in the preheated oven and roast for about 2-2.5 hours or until the internal temperature reaches 145°F (63°C).
- Rest and Slice: Allow the roast to rest for 15 minutes before slicing. Serve with pan drippings.

Notes: The herb and garlic infusion enhances the flavors of the pork loin. Adjust the cooking time based on the size of the roast for optimal results.

Unique twists on classic meat and poultry dishes

In the realm of Italian cuisine, contemporary twists on classic meat and poultry dishes serve as a testament to culinary innovation. Take, for instance, the beloved Bistecca alla Fiorentina, where a modern touch involves a coffee rub applied to the steak before grilling. This unexpected addition imparts a delightful smokiness to the charred exterior, complementing the robust flavor of the Florentine favorite.

Venturing into the realm of Porchetta, a classic roasted pork dish, an imaginative twist emerges with the incorporation of Asian spices. Here, traditional Italian herb blends mingle with notes of star anise and ginger, creating a fusion of aromas and tastes that dance on the taste buds, marrying the old and the new in a succulent harmony.

For those indulging in Arrosto di Maiale, the Italian roast pork, a contemporary rendition might feature a glossy bourbon-infused glaze. This addition introduces a layer of sweetness that beautifully counterbalances the savory richness of the pork, resulting in a symphony of flavors that pays homage to tradition while embracing the spirit of culinary exploration. These reimagined classics invite diners to experience the familiar with a delightful twist, bridging the gap between heritage and innovation on the plate.

Chapter 8

Vegetarian and Vegan Dishes

Importance of vegetarian and vegan dishes in Italian cuisine

The significance of vegetarian and vegan dishes in Italian cuisine is deeply intertwined with the historical, cultural, and geographical tapestry of the country. Embracing a Mediterranean diet, Italians have long understood the harmony between the land and what it provides, giving rise to a plethora of delectable plant-based options.

In traditional Italian households, a multitude of dishes have been inherently vegetarian, stemming from the agricultural roots of "cucina povera." Staples like Ribollita, a hearty Tuscan soup made with vegetables and bread, or Eggplant Parmesan, layered with tomato sauce and mozzarella, exemplify how a bounty of vegetables takes center stage.

Italy's diverse regions contribute unique vegetarian specialties, such as Sicily's Pasta alla Norma, featuring eggplants and tomatoes, or Liguria's iconic Pesto Genovese, showcasing basil, pine nuts, and olive oil. These dishes not only cater to vegetarians but also underscore a philosophy of celebrating seasonal, local produce.

As health-consciousness rises globally, Italian chefs have seamlessly incorporated plant-based elements into their culinary repertoire. Mushroom-based ragùs mimic the richness of meat, while creative combinations like vegan lasagna with cashew cheese or zucchini noodles with pesto showcase a modern, health-centric approach.

Furthermore, the growing awareness of environmental sustainability has spurred a renaissance in plant-centric gastronomy. From vegan pizza options to plant-based gelato, the evolution of Italian cuisine acknowledges the interconnectedness of food choices with ecological well-being.

The importance of vegetarian and vegan dishes in Italian cuisine extends far beyond dietary considerations. It's a testament to the country's agricultural heritage, a celebration of natural flavors, and a response to contemporary values embracing health, ethical choices, and environmental responsibility. As Italy continues to evolve its culinary landscape, plant-based dishes are not just an option but a vibrant and integral part of its gastronomic identity.

Max Mariola's favorite vegetarian and vegan dishes

Pesto
Servings:4
Time Needed: 15 minutes
Ingredients:

- 2 cups fresh basil leaves
- 1/2 cup pine nuts
- 1/2 cup grated Parmesan cheese (skip for vegan version)
- 2-3 garlic cloves
- 1/2 cup extra virgin olive oil
- Salt and pepper to taste

Directions:

- In a food processor, combine basil, pine nuts, garlic, and Parmesan cheese (if using).
- Pulse until ingredients are finely chopped.
- With the processor running, slowly pour in the olive oil until the mixture forms a smooth paste.
- Season with salt and pepper to taste.
- Serve over pasta, as a spread, or a dip.

Notes: For a vegan version, replace Parmesan cheese with nutritional yeast or skip it altogether.

Minestrone

Servings: 6-8
Time Needed: 45 minutes

Ingredients:

- 1 cup diced onion
- 1 cup diced carrots
- 1 cup diced celery
- 3 cloves garlic, minced
- 1 can (15 oz) cannellini beans, drained
- 1 can (15 oz) diced tomatoes
- 1 cup green beans, chopped
- 1/2 cup small pasta
- 6 cups vegetable broth
- 2 teaspoons dried oregano
- Salt and pepper to taste
- 1/4 cup chopped fresh basil

Directions:

- In a large pot, sauté onions, carrots, and celery until softened.
- Add garlic and cook for an additional minute.
- Pour in vegetable broth, diced tomatoes, cannellini beans, green beans, and oregano.
- Bring to a boil, then reduce heat and simmer for 20-25 minutes.
- Add pasta and cook until al dente.

- Season with salt and pepper, stir in fresh basil, and serve.

Notes: Feel free to customize with seasonal vegetables.

Bruschetta

Servings: 4-6
Time Needed: 15 minutes

Ingredients

- 4-5 ripe tomatoes, diced
- 1/4 cup fresh basil, chopped
- 2 cloves garlic, minced
- 2 tablespoons extra virgin olive oil
- Salt and pepper to taste
- Baguette slices, toasted

Directions:

- In a bowl, combine diced tomatoes, basil, garlic, and olive oil.
- Season with salt and pepper, mix well.
- Allow the mixture to marinate for 10 minutes.
- Spoon the tomato mixture onto toasted baguette slices.
- Serve immediately.

Notes: You can add a balsamic glaze drizzle for extra flavor.

Risotto ai Funghi

Servings: 4
Time Needed: 30 minutes

Ingredients:

- 1 1/2 cups Arborio rice
- 1/2 cup dry white wine
- 1/2 cup dried porcini mushrooms, rehydrated
- 4 cups vegetable broth, kept warm
- 1 cup button mushrooms, sliced
- 1/2 cup shallots, finely chopped
- 2 tablespoons olive oil
- 1/2 cup vegan Parmesan cheese
- Salt and pepper to taste
- Fresh parsley, chopped for garnish

Directions:

- In a pan, sauté shallots in olive oil until translucent.
- Add Arborio rice and cook until it becomes translucent around the edges.
- Pour in white wine and cook until it evaporates.
- Begin adding warm vegetable broth, one ladle at a time, stirring constantly until absorbed.

- After 15 minutes, add rehydrated porcini mushrooms and continue the process until rice is creamy.
- In a separate pan, sauté button mushrooms until browned.
- Fold sautéed mushrooms into the risotto, add vegan Parmesan cheese, and season with salt and pepper.
- Garnish with fresh parsley before serving.

Notes: Stirring constantly helps release the rice's starch, creating a creamy texture.

Chapter 9

Desserts

Importance of desserts in Italian cuisine
Desserts hold a special place in Italian cuisine, acting as a sweet finale to a meal and embodying the essence of indulgence and tradition. These treats are more than just sugary delights; they are cultural symbols that reflect Italy's rich history, regional diversity, and the importance of family and communal gatherings.

One of the most iconic Italian desserts is Tiramisu, a layered delicacy made with coffee-soaked ladyfingers, mascarpone cheese, and cocoa. Its name, translating to "pick me up," perfectly encapsulates its role as a mood-enhancing finale to a meal. Tiramisu is a symbol of the creativity and inventiveness inherent in Italian cuisine.

Another classic is Cannoli, originating from Sicily. These tube-shaped pastries are filled with a sweet, creamy ricotta filling and often adorned with candied fruits or chocolate chips. Cannoli showcase the intricate craftsmanship and dedication to flavor that define Italian desserts.

Gelato, the Italian counterpart to ice cream, is renowned worldwide for its velvety texture and intense flavor. It comes in an array of traditional and inventive flavors, showcasing Italy's commitment to using fresh, high-quality ingredients. Gelato is not merely a treat; it's a sensory experience that reflects Italy's dedication to artistry in culinary creations.

Traditional celebrations and holidays often feature Panettone and Pandoro. These sweet bread-like cakes, studded with dried fruits or dusted with powdered sugar, are enjoyed during Christmas and New Year's festivities. Their presence at the table symbolizes warmth, togetherness, and the passing down of familial traditions.

As diverse as the regions of Italy, desserts like Sicilian Cassata, Neapolitan Sfogliatella, and Venetian Torte are rooted in local ingredients and culinary histories. These regional specialties highlight the importance of terroir and the unique flavors of each area.

Italian desserts are not just confections; they are expressions of cultural identity, creativity, and the joy of savoring life's sweet moments. They embody the spirit of Italian cuisine, celebrating tradition, family, and the artistry of crafting memorable culinary experiences. Whether it's a simple biscotto dipped in espresso or an elaborate multi-layered cake, Italian desserts are an integral part of the country's culinary landscape.

Max Mariola's favorite Italian desserts

Sicilian Cassata

Servings: 8-10 slices

Time needed: 2 hours (plus chilling time)

Ingredients:

- 1 sponge cake (store-bought or homemade)
- 500g ricotta cheese
- 200g powdered sugar
- 100g candied fruit, finely chopped
- 50g dark chocolate, grated
- 1/4 cup sweet Marsala wine
- 1 teaspoon vanilla extract
- Icing sugar for dusting

Directions:

- In a large bowl, mix the ricotta cheese with powdered sugar until smooth.
- Add the chopped candied fruit, grated chocolate, Marsala wine, and vanilla extract. Mix well to combine.
- Cut the sponge cake horizontally into three layers.
- Place one layer of the sponge cake in the bottom of a cake mold.
- Spread a portion of the ricotta mixture evenly over the first layer.

- Repeat the process, layering the sponge cake and ricotta mixture until all layers are used, finishing with a layer of ricotta on top.
- Cover the mold with plastic wrap and refrigerate for at least 4 hours or overnight to allow the flavors to meld.
- Before serving, dust the top with icing sugar for a decorative finish.

Notes: Cassata can be customized with your favorite candied fruits and nuts. Adjust the sweetness according to your taste preference.

Neapolitan Sfogliatella

Servings: 12 pastries

Time needed: 1.5 hours

Ingredients:

- 2 sheets of puff pastry (store-bought or homemade)
- 500g ricotta cheese
- 1 cup granulated sugar
- 1/2 cup orange marmalade
- Zest of 1 lemon
- 1 teaspoon cinnamon
- Powdered sugar for dusting

Directions:

- Preheat the oven to 375°F (190°C).
- In a bowl, mix the ricotta cheese, granulated sugar, orange marmalade, lemon zest, and cinnamon until well combined.
- Roll out the puff pastry sheets and cut them into 5x5-inch squares.
- Place a spoonful of the ricotta mixture in the center of each square.
- Fold the pastry over the filling, forming a triangle or shell shape, and press the edges to seal.
- Bake in the preheated oven for 20-25 minutes or until golden brown.
- Allow the sfogliatelle to cool slightly, then dust with powdered sugar before serving.

Notes: Experiment with different fruit fillings or add chopped nuts for variety.

Venetian Torte

Servings: 8 slices

Time needed: 1.5 hours

Ingredients:

- 1 1/2 cups all-purpose flour

- 1 cup granulated sugar
- 1/2 cup unsalted butter, softened
- 1 cup almond flour
- 3 large eggs
- 1/2 cup milk
- Zest of 1 orange
- 1 teaspoon vanilla extract
- Powdered sugar for dusting

Directions:

- Preheat the oven to 350°F (175°C) and grease a cake pan.
- In a bowl, cream together the butter and sugar until light and fluffy.
- Add the eggs one at a time, beating well after each addition.
- Mix in the almond flour, all-purpose flour, milk, orange zest, and vanilla extract until a smooth batter forms.
- Pour the batter into the prepared cake pan.
- Bake for 45-50 minutes or until a toothpick inserted into the center comes out clean.
- Allow the torte to cool in the pan before transferring it to a serving plate.
- Dust with powdered sugar before serving.

Notes: This torte is wonderfully moist and flavorful, making it a delightful treat on its own or with a dollop of whipped cream.

Unique twists on classic Italian desserts

Italian desserts, renowned for their timeless appeal, have recently undergone exciting transformations, introducing inventive twists to beloved classics. Among these, the Hazelnut Tiramisù stands out, replacing the traditional coffee-soaked ladyfingers with layers of hazelnut-flavored sponge cake, creating a symphony of nutty richness. The Cannoli Cheesecake takes inspiration from Sicily's iconic cannoli, featuring a creamy ricotta and mascarpone filling within a buttery graham cracker crust, beautifully merging two beloved treats.

For those seeking a refreshing deviation, the Limoncello Panna Cotta brings a zesty twist to the creamy classic. Infused with the vibrant essence of Limoncello, this dessert presents a perfect marriage of citrusy brightness and silky indulgence. Meanwhile, the Chocolate Olive Oil Mousse presents a bold departure from conventional chocolate mousse, using extra virgin olive oil to impart a luscious texture and an unexpected depth of flavor.

A playful reimagining of the traditional Sicilian Cassata comes in the form of Cassata Ice Cream Sandwiches. This inventive treat features layers of ricotta ice cream, candied fruit, and sponge cake, elegantly sandwiched together, providing a delightful handheld experience of the beloved Sicilian delight.

These contemporary twists on classic Italian desserts showcase the culinary creativity that flourishes within the rich tradition of Italian sweets, offering a new and delightful experience for those with a taste for innovation.

Conclusion

As we draw the curtain on this culinary exploration of Italian gastronomy, it's evident that the essence of Italian cuisine is an intricate tapestry woven with history, passion, and creativity. From the sun-drenched fields of Tuscany to the bustling kitchens of Rome, each region contributes its unique flavors, techniques, and traditions to the rich mosaic that is Italian food.

Our journey began with the foundations of Italian cooking – the simplicity of Max Mariola's philosophy, the rich history of traditional dishes, and the influence of diverse cultures on this gastronomic landscape. We ventured into the contemporary realm, where chefs like Dan Pepperell and Guy Grossi are reshaping classics and introducing exciting, modern twists.

Pasta and risotto emerged as steadfast companions, embodying comfort and versatility. We delved into the significance of seafood, meats, and poultry, discovering their roles in the symphony of Italian flavors. Vegetarian and vegan dishes, often overlooked, revealed themselves as vibrant protagonists, offering a celebration of Italy's bountiful produce.

Desserts, the sweet crescendo of any Italian meal, proved to be an art form in themselves, evolving with inventive twists on cherished classics. From Hazelnut

Tiramisù to Cassata Ice Cream Sandwiches, the world of Italian sweets is as diverse as it is delectable.

This journey wasn't just a culinary exploration; it was a cultural odyssey, a testament to the Italians' profound connection with their land, their traditions, and their love for sharing meals with friends and family. As we close the pages of this gastronomic adventure, let the aromas of basil, the melody of clinking glasses, and the warmth of the Mediterranean sun linger. May this culinary voyage inspire you to embrace the spirit of Italian cooking, infusing every meal with the passion and simplicity that define this extraordinary cuisine.

Buon viaggio culinario!!!

Printed in the USA
CPSIA information can be obtained
at www.ICGtesting.com
LVHW010246250424
778406LV00007B/333